Microsoft Copilot

The Microsoft 365 Companion Series

Dr. Patrick Jones

OLYMPUS ACADEMY
PRESS

TABLE OF CONTENTS

DISCOVERING THE POWER OF MICROSOFT COPILOT

Welcome to the world of Microsoft Copilot! Imagine having a personal digital assistant right there with you, helping you with tasks, answering questions, organizing information, and even offering insights—all within the Microsoft 365 apps you're already using. That's exactly what Copilot is designed to do. It's an AI-powered tool that works alongside you in apps like Word, Excel, Teams, and more, making your work not only easier but also smarter.

So, what exactly is Copilot? Think of it as your productivity partner, a virtual assistant that learns from your work patterns and helps you find information, automate tasks, and get things done faster. For example, imagine you're working on a report in Word—Copilot can pull in data from Excel, draft a summary, or even suggest next steps. It's like having an extra set of hands (or an extra mind) right in your Microsoft apps, ready to support you whenever you need it.

Copilot's biggest strength is its ability to simplify complex tasks. With AI at its core, Copilot doesn't just follow commands—it understands your context, analyzes data, and offers insights based on the information it gathers from your files, emails, chats, and more. This means that instead of juggling multiple tools and trying to keep everything organized on your own, Copilot can help you keep track of everything, anticipate your needs, and offer suggestions. It's about working smarter, not harder.

Imagine saving time on repetitive tasks, having quick access to the information you need, and being able to make data-driven decisions faster. With Copilot, you can focus more on what matters—whether that's connecting with your team, focusing on a project, or simply getting through your day with a little less stress.

This book is here to help you dive into Copilot's features, learn how it works, and discover how to use it in ways that genuinely improve your workflow. We'll start with the basics, like setting up Copilot and understanding where and how it integrates into Microsoft 365. Then, we'll move on to more advanced topics, like automating tasks, summarizing information, and using AI insights to guide your work.

Along the way, you'll follow Sarah's journey as she learns to use Copilot in her daily tasks. Through her experiences, you'll see real-life examples of how Copilot can make a difference—whether it's organizing projects, pulling data from different sources, or finding valuable insights at the right moment. Sarah's story will show you practical ways to use Copilot, making it easier for you to visualize how these features can fit into your own work.

What You'll Gain from This Book

By the end of this guide, you'll be able to:

- **Navigate Copilot's Features**: Get familiar with how Copilot works in various Microsoft 365 apps and learn to access its key features.

- **Automate and Simplify Tasks**: Use Copilot to handle repetitive work, organize data, and even manage communications.

- **Make Data-Driven Decisions**: Learn to tap into Copilot's AI insights, helping you make informed decisions without digging through data manually.

With Copilot as your assistant, you'll find new ways to approach your projects, manage your time, and connect with your team. This guide is here to help you get the most out of Copilot and discover just how powerful it can be in transforming your workflow.

Let's dive in and start exploring all the ways Copilot can support you, inspire you, and make your workday a little easier. Your journey with Microsoft Copilot starts now—let's get started!

WHAT IS COPILOT?

Imagine having a personal assistant right inside your Microsoft 365 apps—an assistant that doesn't just follow commands but actually understands what you need and helps you get there faster. That's Microsoft Copilot. It's a powerful AI-driven tool designed to make your work easier, smarter, and more efficient, whether you're drafting a document in Word, analyzing data in Excel, or connecting with your team in Teams. Copilot is there to help you every step of the way, blending seamlessly into the apps you're already using.

So, what makes Copilot different from a typical tool or feature? Think of it as a digital partner that doesn't just respond to commands—it actually learns from the context of your work. Let's say you're putting together a report. Copilot can pull in data from Excel, summarize trends, suggest next steps, or even create a draft for you. And because it's powered by artificial intelligence, Copilot gets better and more intuitive over time.

Copilot works by tapping into the power of AI, analyzing data from various sources within Microsoft 365, like your documents, spreadsheets, emails, and chats. It uses this information to provide you with relevant suggestions, summaries, or actions that align with your goals. It's as if Copilot has a bird's-eye view of your work and can pull in the right resources or make smart recommendations based on what it sees.

For example, if you're using Word and want to summarize a long document, you can ask Copilot to create a summary for you. In Excel, you might need to analyze sales data—Copilot can help by identifying trends, making calculations, or even suggesting visualizations that make the data easier to understand. And in Teams, Copilot can help with meeting notes, recapping previous discussions, or even drafting messages to keep everyone in the loop.

The real magic of Copilot lies in its ability to reduce the time you spend on repetitive tasks and help you focus on the things that truly matter. Here's how Copilot brings unique value to your workflow:

- **Automating Tedious Tasks**: From summarizing data to generating drafts, Copilot can handle those routine tasks that often take up too much of your time.

- **Providing Smart Suggestions**: Copilot's AI doesn't just wait for you to ask questions—it actively offers suggestions based on the work you're doing, helping you move forward faster.

- **Connecting Information Seamlessly**: Because it has access to all your Microsoft 365 apps, Copilot can bring together data and insights from multiple sources, saving you the hassle of jumping between apps.

Think of Copilot as your productivity sidekick, someone who's always there to lend a hand when you need it. Instead of searching through files, organizing data, or drafting updates from scratch, you can turn to Copilot to do the heavy lifting. It's like having an extra pair of hands and an extra brain, all within the apps you're already comfortable with. The result? More time for you to focus on the creative and strategic parts of your work.

So, at its core, Microsoft Copilot isn't just a feature—it's a smarter, more intuitive way to work. With Copilot by your side, you can simplify complex tasks, make informed decisions faster, and bring a new level of ease to your everyday projects. It's there to make your workday smoother, helping you get more done with less effort. Now that's a tool worth having.

WHY USE COPILOT?

So, why should you use Microsoft Copilot? Imagine having an intelligent assistant right in your Microsoft 365 apps that not only helps you stay organized but actually understands your goals, supports your projects, and makes your work smoother. Copilot isn't just a tool—it's a game-changer, designed to take the guesswork out of managing information, handling tasks, and making decisions.

Here's why Copilot could be exactly what you've been looking for to elevate your productivity and keep you focused on what matters most.

1. Save Time on Repetitive Tasks

Let's face it: some tasks can be, well, a bit tedious. Maybe it's summarizing long documents, organizing files, or pulling together data from multiple sources. These tasks often eat up valuable time that could be spent on more impactful work. Copilot steps in to take care of these repetitive chores, allowing you to delegate the busywork. Need a quick summary? Want a chart for your data? Copilot's got it covered. By handling routine tasks, it gives you time back to focus on the bigger picture.

2. Make Smarter, Data-Driven Decisions

One of the hardest parts of working with large amounts of information is figuring out what's important. Copilot helps with this by gathering, analyzing, and even interpreting data across your Microsoft 365 apps. Let's say you're working in Excel and want insights on sales data— Copilot can highlight trends, suggest patterns, or recommend next steps based on the numbers. It doesn't just present data; it helps you make sense of it, which can lead to better, more informed decisions.

3. Collaborate Effortlessly

When it comes to teamwork, Copilot shines. It streamlines collaboration by keeping everyone on the same page, helping you organize information and communicate effectively. In Teams, for instance, Copilot can summarize previous meeting notes, suggest relevant files, or even draft updates for you to share with your team. This makes staying connected and in sync with others much simpler, so you can spend less time coordinating and more time moving projects forward.

4. Enjoy a More Personalized Experience

Unlike a one-size-fits-all tool, Copilot learns from how you work. It pays attention to your preferences, the types of tasks you handle, and the apps you use most often. This means that over time, Copilot tailors its suggestions and actions to fit your unique workflow, making it feel like a personalized assistant. Need reminders for a specific project? Copilot will start to anticipate that. Often work with certain files? Copilot can bring those to the surface faster.

5. Reduce Information Overload

In today's digital world, it's easy to feel overwhelmed by the sheer volume of information we deal with daily. Copilot acts like a filter, pulling out the details that are actually relevant to you and organizing them in a way that's easy to digest. Whether it's summarizing a long email thread, highlighting key points in a document, or suggesting resources for a project, Copilot helps you manage information without getting bogged down.

6. Boost Creativity and Innovation

By handling routine tasks and organizing information, Copilot frees up your mental energy for creative thinking and problem-solving. Instead of getting lost in the weeds, you can focus on the big ideas, the strategic decisions, and the parts of your work that require real creativity. And when you do need some inspiration, Copilot can even suggest ideas, make recommendations, or offer insights that spark new directions.

7. Work Flexibly Across Devices

Whether you're at your desk, on a tablet, or checking things on your phone, Copilot is there. Since it's integrated across Microsoft 365, Copilot's help is never more than a click away. You can rely on it to pull in files, remind you of important dates, or update you on project progress from anywhere, making it easy to keep working on the go.

8. Streamline Project Management

Keeping track of all the moving parts in a project can be challenging, but Copilot simplifies this. It can help you manage deadlines, prioritize tasks, and keep track of details without needing multiple tools or complex planning systems. With Copilot, you have a built-in project assistant that can organize information, set reminders, and even keep your team updated automatically.

In short, Copilot takes on the heavy lifting so you can focus on what's important. By streamlining tasks, organizing information, and providing insights, it transforms the way you work, helping you stay on top of your projects with less effort and more confidence. So if you're ready to work smarter, save time, and make informed decisions without the stress, Copilot is here to help you do just that.

HOW TO GET STARTED

Getting started with Microsoft Copilot is easier than you might think, and once it's set up, you'll have a powerful assistant right inside your favorite Microsoft 365 apps. Whether you're new to AI tools or just looking to dive into Copilot's features, this guide will help you get up and running in no time. Let's walk through the basics so you can start making the most of what Copilot has to offer.

1. Make Sure You Have Access to Microsoft Copilot

The first step is to make sure your account has access. Check with your IT department, the Microsoft 365 admin for your organization, or your account information if you're not sure. While the general Copilot app is free to use, Copilot within your Microsoft 365 apps requires a license to enable Copilot, so it's always good to verify.

2. Enable Copilot in Your Microsoft 365 Settings

Once Copilot is activated, you'll see it appear in various apps with prompts or tips to get started. Think of it as a gentle guide introducing you to the possibilities.

3. Familiarize Yourself with Copilot's Interface

Now that Copilot is enabled, let's get comfortable with how it looks and works. You'll usually find Copilot's features in the ribbon, the toolbar or as a sidebar within each app.

- **Look for the Copilot Icon**: In many apps, Copilot has its own icon or panel. This is where you can interact with Copilot, ask questions, or view suggested actions.

- **Explore the Sidebar**: When you open Copilot in an app like Word or Excel, a sidebar may pop up with options and suggestions. This is your main workspace with Copilot, so feel free to explore and click around!

4. Start with Simple Commands

The best way to get used to Copilot is to start small. Try asking it to do something simple and see how it responds.

- **Example Commands**: Try phrases like "Summarize this document," "Create a chart from this data," or "Draft an email response." These basic commands are great for learning how Copilot interprets your instructions and getting a feel for its capabilities.

- **Explore Suggestions**: In many apps, Copilot will automatically offer suggestions based on what you're doing. Take advantage of these—they're often handy tips that can make your work easier!

5. Use Copilot in Different Apps

One of the great things about Copilot is its versatility across Microsoft 365. Each app uses Copilot a little differently, so exploring multiple apps can help you discover the full range of what it can do.

- **In Word**: Copilot can assist with drafting, editing, and summarizing text. Try having it draft an outline or suggest edits to polish your writing.

- **In Excel**: Copilot shines in data analysis. Ask it to create charts, analyze trends, or suggest insights from your data.

- **In Teams**: Use Copilot to summarize chat threads, prepare meeting notes, or suggest follow-up actions for your team.

- **In Outlook:** Let Copilot help with drafting emails, setting reminders, or sorting through messages to find what's most important.

Each app offers unique ways to interact with Copilot, so spend a few minutes experimenting with commands and suggestions in each one.

6. Explore Advanced Features

Once you're comfortable with the basics, it's time to dive into Copilot's more advanced features.

- **Automate Routine Tasks:** If you have tasks you do regularly, try creating automation commands in Copilot. For instance, you can set it up to generate reports, summarize long documents, or pull key metrics from spreadsheets.

- **Use Copilot's Insights and Recommendations:** In apps like Excel and Word, Copilot doesn't just follow commands; it offers data-driven insights and recommendations. Tap into these to make more informed decisions without digging through tons of data.

7. Customize Copilot for Your Workflow

Copilot can adapt to your specific needs and preferences over time. You can adjust settings, commands, and even some aspects of how Copilot interacts with your files.

- **Adjust Copilot's Preferences:** In your app settings, look for preferences related to Copilot. You can often customize what type of suggestions it offers or how it displays information.

- **Teach Copilot Your Patterns:** Copilot learns from your work style, so as you use it, it'll start tailoring suggestions based on your habits. The more you use Copilot, the more relevant its suggestions become!

8. Take Advantage of Copilot's Learning Resources

Microsoft offers resources, tutorials, and tips directly within Copilot and through their website. These resources are there to help you understand new features, explore best practices, and make the most of Copilot's capabilities.

- **In-App Tips and Hints**: Look for tooltips and hints that pop up in the sidebar or as you explore commands—these often provide helpful insights on using Copilot more effectively.

- **Visit the Microsoft Copilot Help Center**: Microsoft has online resources specifically for Copilot. If you're ever curious about a feature or need guidance, the Help Center is a great place to find step-by-step instructions and FAQs.

With these steps, you're ready to start using Microsoft Copilot and making it a valuable part of your daily workflow. The best way to learn is by doing, so don't hesitate to try new commands, explore features, and let Copilot guide you through its many possibilities. Remember, Copilot is here to make your work easier, support your goals, and give you back time for the tasks that matter most.

Dive in, experiment, and watch how Copilot transforms the way you work—one helpful suggestion at a time.

PROMPTING

One of the best ways to unlock the full potential of Microsoft Copilot is by mastering the art of prompting. Think of prompting as giving Copilot the right "instructions" to get the best results. Since Copilot is powered by AI, it responds to your input—so the more clearly you ask, the better Copilot can understand what you need.

1. Be Clear and Specific with Your Requests

One of the simplest ways to get the best results from Copilot is to be as clear and specific as possible. Instead of vague requests, try to add a little more detail so Copilot knows exactly what you're looking for.

- **Vague Prompt**: "Summarize this report."
- **Clear Prompt**: "Summarize the key findings of this report in three bullet points."

By specifying that you want "key findings" and in "three bullet points," you give Copilot clear directions that help it create a more focused, useful response.

2. Break Down Complex Tasks into Smaller Steps

If you're asking Copilot for help with something complex, it can sometimes help to break down your request into smaller parts. This way, you're guiding Copilot step-by-step, which can lead to more accurate results.

- **Single Complex Prompt**: "Analyze this data for trends and create a report with charts."
- **Step-by-Step Prompts**: Start with "Identify any trends in this data," then ask "Create charts that represent these trends," and finally, "Generate a summary report based on the charts."

Breaking down tasks also gives you more control, allowing you to adjust and refine as you go along.

3. Use Context to Guide Copilot's Responses

Copilot can draw on data and files within your Microsoft 365 apps, but it's always helpful to give it some context so it knows which specific information is most relevant to you. If you're working with several documents or datasets, a bit of context can go a long way.

- **Without Context**: "Provide insights on this project."

- **With Context**: "Using data from the sales report in Excel, provide insights on this project's revenue trends for the past quarter."

By telling Copilot to use the "sales report in Excel" and focusing on "revenue trends for the past quarter," you're steering it toward the right information and avoiding irrelevant details.

4. Experiment with Different Wording

If Copilot's response isn't quite what you expected, try rephrasing your prompt. Sometimes a small change in wording can lead to a big difference in results. Don't be afraid to try out different ways of asking the same thing to see which one works best.

- **Initial Prompt**: "Explain this data."

- **Revised Prompt**: "Can you break down the main points of this data in simple terms?" or "Summarize the most important trends in this data for a presentation."

Experimenting with phrasing helps you find the prompts that best align with Copilot's understanding, giving you responses that match your needs more closely.

5. Use Action Words to Direct Copilot's Output

When you're asking Copilot for help, action words can make your prompt more effective by specifying what you want to accomplish. Words like "summarize," "analyze," "list," "compare," and "highlight" give Copilot a clear action to take, making its response more targeted.

- **Prompt**: "Compare this year's revenue with last year's and highlight the main differences."

- **Result**: Copilot will know to look for differences in revenue data and bring them to the surface.

Action words help Copilot focus on the type of response you're after, leading to results that are directly useful.

6. Ask Follow-Up Questions

If Copilot's initial response is helpful but you want a little more detail, go ahead and ask follow-up questions. You can treat Copilot as if you're having a conversation, refining and expanding on what you've already received.

- **Initial Prompt**: "Summarize the main points of this report."

- **Follow-Up Prompt**: "Can you provide a few examples from the report to support these points?"

Follow-up prompts let you dig deeper without starting from scratch, making it easy to get more specific information as you refine your needs.

7. Set Formatting Preferences in Your Prompts

When asking Copilot to generate content, you can specify your preferred format—like bullet points, paragraphs, or lists. This helps Copilot deliver responses that are not only informative but also easy to incorporate into your work.

- **Prompt with Formatting**: "Summarize this document's findings in bullet points."

- **Another Example**: "Provide a three-paragraph overview of this proposal."

Specifying the format gives you ready-to-use content that fits seamlessly into your documents or presentations.

8. Include Timeframes or Other Relevant Details

If your request involves data, documents, or events that are time-sensitive, mention the relevant timeframes. This keeps Copilot focused on the most current or relevant information, avoiding outdated data.

- **Without Timeframe**: "What are the top sales trends?"

- **With Timeframe**: "What are the top sales trends for the past six months?"

A timeframe helps Copilot filter through your data and deliver insights that are timely and relevant to your current projects.

Getting comfortable with prompting is key to making the most of Microsoft Copilot. By being specific, using action words, and refining your prompts, you'll help Copilot understand exactly what you need, making your experience with it more productive and efficient. Remember, Copilot is designed to respond to your instructions—so the clearer you are, the more helpful it can be.

Prompting effectively is a skill you'll build over time. Don't be afraid to experiment, ask follow-up questions, and see how different prompts impact the responses you get. With a little practice, you'll be able to communicate with Copilot in a way that feels natural and get the results you need faster and more accurately.

BEST PRACTICES

Now that you're familiar with Copilot's capabilities, let's look at some best practices to make the most of this powerful tool. Copilot is here to make your work easier, but with a few thoughtful approaches, you can ensure that it consistently delivers the results you're looking for. These tips will help you keep your workflow smooth, your data secure, and your experience with Copilot as productive as possible.

1. Start Simple and Build Up

When you're getting started, keep your prompts simple and direct. Begin with basic requests to get a feel for how Copilot responds, and then gradually build up to more complex tasks.

- **Example**: Instead of jumping into a detailed report request, start with, "Summarize this document," and then follow up with, "Add more details about section two."

- **Why It Helps**: Starting simple helps you get comfortable with Copilot's responses, making it easier to refine prompts as you go.

2. Take Advantage of Copilot's Suggestions

Copilot often provides suggestions based on your current activity. Don't ignore these hints—they're tailored to help you work more effectively based on what you're doing.

- **Example**: In Word, Copilot might suggest summarizing sections of a long document or editing grammar. In Excel, it might offer to create charts from your data.

- **Why It Helps**: These suggestions save you time by highlighting useful actions, especially if you're working on repetitive or time-sensitive tasks.

3. Make Use of Data Insights for Better Decisions

One of Copilot's standout features is its ability to analyze and interpret data. If you're working in Excel or Word with complex data sets, ask Copilot for insights that go beyond basic calculations.

- **Example**: "Analyze the quarterly sales data for trends" or "Suggest insights based on recent sales figures."

- **Why It Helps**: Copilot's analysis can highlight trends, outliers, or patterns, helping you make data-driven decisions without having to dig through numbers manually.

4. Customize Copilot Settings to Fit Your Workflow

Copilot is designed to be flexible, so take some time to adjust settings to suit your preferences. You can control how often Copilot provides suggestions, the type of insights it highlights, and its general interaction style.

- **Example**: In your Microsoft 365 settings, look for Copilot preferences, where you can adjust suggestion frequency or choose which types of insights Copilot should focus on.

- **Why It Helps**: Customizing Copilot means that it will give you the types of help you find most useful, making your workflow smoother and more tailored to your needs.

5. Maintain Security and Privacy with Sensitive Data

When using Copilot, especially in collaborative settings, it's essential to keep security and privacy top of mind. Be mindful of sensitive information and control access to files with confidential data.

- **Example**: Use Copilot's "Specific People" sharing settings in Teams or restrict access to sensitive documents in Word and Excel.
- **Why It Helps**: By keeping a close eye on data security, you can confidently use Copilot in professional or confidential settings without risking unintended data exposure.

6. Use Version History as a Backup

If you're making significant changes to a document with Copilot's help, make use of the version history feature in Word, Excel, or other apps. This way, if you need to revert to an earlier version, it's easy to do.

- **Example**: Right-click on a document in OneDrive or SharePoint and select "Version History" to see previous versions.
- **Why It Helps**: Version history acts as a safety net, allowing you to experiment with Copilot's suggestions without worrying about permanently altering the original content.

7. Combine Copilot with Other Microsoft 365 Features

Copilot works well with other Microsoft 365 tools, so don't hesitate to integrate its insights with other features. For example, use Copilot's summaries and insights in Word to prepare for meetings in Teams or share its analysis from Excel in a PowerPoint presentation.

- **Example**: Use Copilot to summarize a project's key points in Word, then share that summary as a OneNote entry for team collaboration.
- **Why It Helps**: Integrating Copilot with other tools helps create a seamless workflow, ensuring that insights and data flow smoothly across projects and teams.

8. Prompt Thoughtfully and Use Follow-Ups

Copilot's responses are only as good as the prompts you give it, so keep your prompts clear and specific. And remember, follow-up questions are a great way to refine and deepen Copilot's responses.

- **Example**: Start with "Summarize this report," then follow up with, "Can you include some examples from section two?"

- **Why It Helps**: Prompting thoughtfully allows Copilot to understand exactly what you need, and follow-ups let you get more nuanced information without starting from scratch.

9. Review Suggestions Before Accepting

Copilot is designed to make your work easier, but it's still essential to review its suggestions before implementing them. This ensures the content aligns with your intentions and avoids any potential misinterpretations.

- **Example**: In Word, if Copilot suggests edits, take a quick look to make sure the tone and accuracy fit your document's purpose.

- **Why It Helps**: A quick review helps maintain quality and consistency, giving you control over the final output.

10. Keep Experimenting and Learning

Copilot is a flexible, learning AI that becomes even more effective the more you use it. Don't hesitate to try new commands, explore additional features, and see how it can adapt to different tasks.

- **Example**: Experiment with asking Copilot to summarize, suggest insights, or even help plan out tasks across different apps.

- **Why It Helps**: By continually exploring, you'll find new ways Copilot can support your workflow and discover unexpected features that make your work easier.

Using these best practices, you can make the most of Microsoft Copilot, transforming it from just another feature into a genuinely valuable assistant in your daily work. From crafting clear prompts to taking advantage of its data insights and integrations, these tips will help you work smarter, save time, and stay organized. Remember, Copilot is there to make your work more efficient and enjoyable, so lean into its capabilities, keep experimenting, and enjoy the benefits of having a digital assistant by your side.

TIPS AND TRICKS

Now that you're familiar with the basics of Microsoft Copilot and some best practices, let's dive into a few tips and tricks to truly maximize its potential. These tips will help you work smarter, personalize your experience, and uncover some of Copilot's hidden features. Think of this as your toolkit for getting the best results from Copilot—every time you use it.

1. Use Shortcuts for Quick Commands

When you're in a hurry, using shortcuts can make interacting with Copilot even faster. Many apps offer quick access commands or keyboard shortcuts to activate Copilot features, allowing you to save time and jump right into action.

Example: In Word or Excel, you can use a keyboard shortcut to quickly bring up Copilot and start a prompt.

Why It Helps: Shortcuts let you access Copilot features instantly, which is especially helpful when you're working on a tight deadline.

2. Ask for Recommendations and Insights, Not Just Tasks

Copilot can provide recommendations and insights based on your data, not just perform tasks. So, if you're unsure what's next in a project or want some guidance, try asking Copilot for its suggestions.

Prompt Example: "What are the top trends in this data?" or "Can you suggest next steps based on this report?"

Why It Helps: This approach takes advantage of Copilot's AI capabilities, giving you new ideas or uncovering information you might have missed.

3. Use Copilot's Formatting Capabilities

If you're creating documents, presentations, or emails, Copilot can help with formatting as well as content. You can prompt it to apply specific formats, styles, or layouts to keep things visually appealing and easy to read.

Example: "Format this document in a professional style" or "Organize these points into bullet points."

Why It Helps: This saves time on formatting, especially when preparing materials for presentations or reports.

4. Turn On Notifications for Copilot Suggestions

Copilot can offer real-time suggestions as you work. By enabling notifications, you can stay updated on Copilot's insights without actively searching for them.

How to Enable: Go to your app's settings and enable notifications for Copilot. This is particularly useful in Teams, where Copilot can provide suggestions during meetings or while reviewing chat threads.

Why It Helps: Notifications keep you in the loop without interrupting your workflow, letting Copilot prompt you with helpful information at just the right time.

5. Leverage Copilot for Meeting Prep and Follow-Up

Copilot is a great tool for both preparing for meetings and handling follow-up tasks afterward. Use it to organize agendas, summarize meeting notes, or draft follow-up emails.

Example: In Teams, ask Copilot to "Create a summary of key points from today's meeting" or "Draft an email follow-up based on the discussion."

Why It Helps: This simplifies meeting management and helps you stay organized without spending extra time on prep or wrap-up tasks.

6. Use Copilot to Simplify Data Analysis

If you're working with data, Copilot can go beyond simple calculations. Ask it to highlight trends, compare data points, or create visualizations that make your data easier to understand at a glance.

Example: "Identify the top 3 trends in this sales data" or "Create a pie chart showing product distribution."

Why It Helps: This makes data analysis accessible, even if you're not an Excel expert, allowing you to make sense of complex data quickly.

7. Ask Copilot to Improve or Edit Text

If you're working on a document, email, or presentation, Copilot can help refine your text for clarity, grammar, and style. This is particularly useful if you want a second opinion on a draft or need a quick polish.

Prompt Example: "Edit this paragraph for clarity" or "Make this email sound more professional."

Why It Helps: Editing assistance can give you a fresh perspective, helping you communicate more effectively without spending time on manual edits.

8. Take Advantage of Contextual Suggestions

Copilot can recognize the context of what you're working on, offering helpful suggestions based on your specific tasks. Pay attention to these contextual suggestions—they're designed to fit naturally with your current work.

Example: While reviewing a document, Copilot might suggest summarizing it, adding bullet points, or highlighting key points.

Why It Helps: Contextual suggestions are tailored to what you're already doing, making it easy to incorporate Copilot's help without disrupting your workflow.

9. Create Task Lists and Organize Projects with Copilot

In addition to individual tasks, Copilot can help you create and organize task lists, project plans, and even timelines, making it a handy tool for project management.

Example: "Create a task list for this project" or "Organize these steps into a project timeline."

Why It Helps: With task lists and timelines, Copilot can help you keep track of project details, deadlines, and progress without needing separate project management software.

10. Ask for Explanations When Needed

If you're ever unsure about a Copilot suggestion or need clarity on data insights, don't hesitate to ask Copilot for an explanation. This can be helpful in understanding data results or unfamiliar terms.

Prompt Example: "Explain why you highlighted this trend" or "What does this term mean in this context?"

Why It Helps: Getting explanations helps deepen your understanding and builds your confidence in using Copilot's insights.

11. Use Copilot to Automate Repetitive Tasks

For tasks you perform regularly, Copilot can help streamline these processes by setting up automated workflows. This is especially useful in apps like Excel, where you may have repetitive data entry or analysis tasks.

Example: "Create a formula to calculate monthly totals" or "Automate a summary of each new entry."

Why It Helps: Automation frees up time by handling repetitive tasks, letting you focus on more strategic work.

12. Keep Experimenting and Exploring New Features

Microsoft frequently updates Copilot's capabilities, so keep an eye out for new features. Experimenting with these updates can help you discover new ways Copilot can enhance your work.

Example: Try out new prompts or explore advanced features as they're released, like document summarization improvements or new insights in Excel.

Why It Helps: Staying curious about updates keeps you ahead of the curve, ensuring you're always getting the most out of Copilot's evolving features.

With these tips and tricks, you're well on your way to becoming a Microsoft Copilot pro. Remember, Copilot is designed to be flexible, adaptable, and responsive to your needs—so don't hesitate to try new commands, explore different prompts, and let Copilot support your workflow in creative ways. Whether you're using it to streamline your meetings, analyze data, or polish a presentation, these tips will help you make Copilot a valuable part of your digital toolkit.

COMMON PITFALLS AND HOW TO AVOID THEM

Microsoft Copilot can be a powerful tool when used effectively, but there are a few common pitfalls that can impact its usefulness if you're not aware of them. Let's explore these pitfalls and offer practical solutions to help you avoid them, ensuring that your experience with Copilot remains productive, secure, and frustration-free.

1. Relying Too Heavily on Copilot for Critical Decisions

Pitfall:
While Copilot is excellent for providing data insights, summaries, and recommendations, it's still an AI tool and not a human decision-maker. Relying on it entirely for major decisions can be risky, as it may not account for all the nuances involved in complex issues.

How to Avoid It:

- **Use Copilot's Insights as a Starting Point**: Treat Copilot's suggestions as helpful guidance but add your own judgment and expertise to make final decisions.

- **Review Suggestions Carefully**: Especially with sensitive or complex matters, double-check Copilot's insights to ensure they align with your goals.

Copilot's insights can be a great resource, but remember that it's there to support your decisions, not replace them.

2. Overlooking Security and Privacy When Sharing Data

Pitfall:
Copilot pulls information from various Microsoft 365 apps to help you, which means it has access to your documents, spreadsheets, and emails.

If you're not careful, this can lead to accidental exposure of sensitive data, especially in shared or collaborative settings.

How to Avoid It:

- **Control File Access**: When sharing files or allowing Copilot to access sensitive information, use specific permissions to restrict access to only those who need it.

- **Double-Check Permissions**: Before sharing Copilot-generated content, make sure it doesn't include sensitive information unintentionally pulled from other sources.

Keeping security top of mind ensures that you use Copilot responsibly and avoid accidental data leaks.

3. Using Vague Prompts and Getting Unfocused Results

Pitfall:
If your prompts to Copilot are too vague, you might get responses that don't meet your needs or are filled with irrelevant information. This can lead to frustration or wasted time refining Copilot's output.

How to Avoid It:

- **Be Specific and Clear in Your Prompts**: Use detailed prompts that specify what you're looking for, whether that's a summary, a specific analysis, or a type of formatting.

- **Guide Copilot with Follow-Up Prompts**: If the first response isn't quite right, try refining your prompt with more specifics or ask Copilot to narrow its focus.

Clear, detailed prompting is key to getting the most relevant and accurate responses from Copilot.

4. Ignoring Suggested Insights and Missing Opportunities

Pitfall:

Copilot's suggestions are designed to help you work smarter, but if you overlook these insights or dismiss them too quickly, you could miss out on valuable information or opportunities to improve your workflow.

How to Avoid It:

- **Take a Moment to Review Suggestions**: Even if you don't use every suggestion, a quick review of Copilot's prompts can reveal useful shortcuts or insights.

- **Experiment with Different Prompts**: Don't be afraid to try out new prompts or explore areas where Copilot might offer insights. You may discover useful features that you hadn't considered.

Embracing Copilot's suggestions with an open mind can reveal new ways to boost your productivity.

5. Not Customizing Copilot Settings to Match Your Workflow

Pitfall:

Copilot's default settings may not perfectly align with how you work. If you leave these settings untouched, you might miss out on a more tailored, efficient experience.

How to Avoid It:

- **Adjust Copilot's Preferences**: Explore the settings in your Microsoft 365 apps to adjust how often Copilot provides suggestions, the types of insights it offers, and its interaction style.

- **Use the Tools That Suit Your Needs**: For instance, if you're more focused on analysis than on writing, prioritize Copilot's features in Excel. Adjusting these preferences lets you shape Copilot's role to better fit your workflow.

Customizing Copilot's settings helps you get the most out of the tool by aligning it with your specific work needs.

6. Forgetting to Review and Edit Copilot's Output

Pitfall:
It's tempting to accept Copilot's suggestions at face value, but remember that Copilot isn't perfect. Accepting output without review can lead to minor errors, misinterpretations, or content that doesn't quite match your intended tone.

How to Avoid It:

- **Always Review Before Finalizing**: Before sharing or publishing Copilot's work, read through its suggestions to ensure accuracy and alignment with your goals.

- **Use Edits to Improve Tone and Clarity**: Copilot can provide a solid draft, but a quick edit by you can refine it to better fit your style and message.

A quick review of Copilot's output ensures it meets your standards and saves you from unintended errors.

7. Overloading Copilot with Too Many Tasks at Once

Pitfall:
If you ask Copilot to handle too many tasks simultaneously, it may produce incomplete or confusing results. Copilot works best when it has a clear, focused direction for each task.

How to Avoid It:

- **Break Down Large Tasks into Smaller Prompts**: Instead of one large request, ask for each part separately to keep Copilot focused.

- **Tackle Tasks One Step at a Time**: Use follow-up prompts to build on the initial output and move gradually toward your end goal.

This step-by-step approach gives Copilot the clarity it needs to deliver the best results.

8. Relying Solely on Copilot and Missing Out on Learning

Pitfall:

While Copilot can help you work more efficiently, relying on it entirely for every task could prevent you from building valuable skills or learning new features of Microsoft 365 on your own.

How to Avoid It:

- **Use Copilot as a Learning Tool**: When Copilot performs a task, pay attention to how it does it. This can help you learn techniques you can apply on your own.

- **Challenge Yourself with Manual Tasks**: Occasionally try performing tasks manually to reinforce your knowledge and keep your skills sharp.

Treating Copilot as a learning partner, not just a tool, can enhance your skills and deepen your understanding of Microsoft 365.

By being aware of these common pitfalls and using these strategies to avoid them, you can make Copilot a valuable, effective part of your daily workflow. Whether it's using clear prompts, staying mindful of security, or reviewing output carefully, these tips ensure you get the best results from Copilot while keeping your data safe and your work on track.

With these insights, you're ready to tackle your projects confidently, knowing how to make Copilot work for you in the most productive, efficient way possible. Let's continue exploring Copilot's potential while keeping an eye out for these easy-to-avoid pitfalls!

SARAH'S FIRST DAY WITH MICROSOFT COPILOT

Sarah sighed as she looked over her long to-do list. Reports to finish, emails to respond to, a presentation to prepare—there never seemed to be enough hours in the day. She had heard about Microsoft Copilot, an AI assistant integrated within the Microsoft 365 apps she already used, but she hadn't explored it much beyond its initial setup. Today, however, Sarah was determined to give it a try and see if it could actually make her day easier.

Her first task of the day was to draft a quarterly report. Sarah opened Microsoft Word, clicked on the "Copilot" tab in the ribbon, and tentatively clicked on "Generate Content." She typed in her prompt: "Draft an introduction for a quarterly sales report aimed at upper management."

Within moments, Copilot generated a few sentences, pulling together relevant data and setting a professional tone. Sarah scanned the content and felt relieved—while it wasn't perfect, it was a solid start, something she could quickly polish and build on.

Impressed by how quickly Copilot created the introduction, she continued asking for support, prompting it with, "Add a summary of the most significant sales growth trends this quarter." Copilot provided a short paragraph highlighting key data points. Sarah made a few tweaks and realized that, for the first time, she was making fast progress on her report without struggling to find the right words.

Next, Sarah needed to analyze a large dataset in Excel. Sales figures, product performance, and customer demographics were all part of the spreadsheet, but spotting meaningful patterns was time-consuming. She selected the data range and typed, "Copilot, analyze this data and summarize key trends."

In seconds, Copilot returned a summary of the data, pointing out patterns she hadn't noticed, like the increase in customer engagement among specific demographics. Sarah then prompted, "Generate a bar chart for top-performing products," and watched as Copilot created a polished chart she could insert directly into her report.

For the first time, data analysis didn't feel overwhelming. With Copilot's help, Sarah could focus on interpreting the insights rather than getting bogged down in the manual process of organizing and visualizing data.

After finishing her report draft, Sarah turned her attention to her overflowing inbox. The thought of going through dozens of emails felt daunting, but Copilot was already there, offering summaries of long email threads. Sarah selected one particularly lengthy exchange, a chain of emails between departments discussing a new product launch. "Copilot, summarize the key points from this thread," she prompted.

The AI assistant condensed the emails into a concise overview, highlighting the main takeaways and action items. She quickly scanned through, noted the key points, and felt confident she understood the entire thread without needing to read each message.

When she needed to respond to a client inquiry, Sarah prompted Copilot again, asking it to draft a professional response based on previous similar emails. Copilot's suggested reply saved her time and gave her a framework to build on, so she could respond quickly without starting from scratch.

As the day went on, Sarah joined a project meeting in Microsoft Teams. During the discussion, she noticed Copilot was quietly capturing key points and generating a meeting summary in real-time. At the end of the meeting, she asked, "Copilot, list the action items from today's discussion." Copilot returned a clear list of follow-up tasks, complete with deadlines and assigned responsibilities.

With everyone on the same page, Sarah realized she wouldn't need to write a lengthy recap email or worry about missed points. Copilot's summary provided a reliable reference for the team, ensuring they could jump right into their assigned tasks.

She also used Copilot's suggestion to draft an agenda for the next meeting. By prompting, "Generate an agenda for the project update meeting next week," Copilot produced a draft based on their current project progress, letting Sarah finalize it in seconds.

By the end of the day, Sarah was amazed at how much she had accomplished. With Copilot's help, she had drafted her quarterly report, analyzed data, stayed on top of email threads, and organized her team's tasks—all in a fraction of the time it usually took her.

As she closed her laptop, her manager approached her. "Sarah, I noticed you wrapped up that report quickly. Would you be willing to share your tips with the team in our next meeting?"

Sarah smiled, knowing exactly what her first tip would be: "Start using Copilot. It's like having an extra set of hands to help with the heavy lifting."

With Copilot by her side, Sarah felt more productive and confident. She was excited to explore even more ways to leverage it, and she couldn't wait to help her colleagues experience the same productivity boost. The journey had only just begun.

EMBRACING THE POWER OF COPILOT

It's clear that Microsoft Copilot is much more than just a tool—it's a game-changing assistant that can transform the way you work, learn, and grow. From organizing data to helping you draft documents, Copilot is here to make your workday smoother, smarter, and more productive. Let's take a quick look back at what we've covered and reflect on how this journey relates to both Sarah's story and your own path to embracing Copilot.

Through this guide, we explored how Copilot can serve as a powerful assistant across various Microsoft 365 apps. Here's a recap of the essential features and practices that can help you make the most of Copilot:

- **Understanding Copilot**: Copilot is an AI-driven tool that integrates with Microsoft 365, helping you with tasks, insights, and automation across apps like Word, Excel, Teams, and Outlook.

- **Why Use Copilot**: Copilot saves time on repetitive tasks, offers data-driven insights, streamlines collaboration, and personalizes suggestions to match your work style, making it invaluable for both individual productivity and team collaboration.

- **Getting Started**: Setting up Copilot and exploring its basic features in different apps lays the groundwork for productive use. Starting with small, clear prompts helps you ease into its capabilities and discover its strengths.

- **Effective Prompting**: Crafting clear, specific prompts allows you to guide Copilot effectively, ensuring you get the responses you need. Breaking down complex tasks and using follow-up prompts helps Copilot deliver more accurate and useful results.

- **Best Practices**: Applying best practices—such as reviewing outputs, personalizing settings, and using contextual suggestions—helps you make the most of Copilot while keeping your data secure and your work efficient.

- **Tips and Tricks**: Shortcuts, insights, formatting requests, and follow-up questions are among the tips that can make Copilot even more helpful and tailored to your workflow.

- **Avoiding Common Pitfalls**: Being aware of pitfalls, like relying too heavily on Copilot for critical decisions or overlooking privacy settings, ensures that you use Copilot safely and responsibly.

Together, these insights equip you to use Copilot confidently, transforming it from just another feature into a trusted digital partner.

We followed Sarah's journey as she learned to use Copilot to support her work. At first, she approached Copilot with curiosity but perhaps a little uncertainty. We saw Sarah explore new features, refine her prompts, and discover the ways Copilot could simplify her tasks, spark ideas, and enhance her productivity. Sarah's journey is a mirror of the learning curve that anyone new to Copilot might experience—beginning with the basics, building confidence, and ultimately transforming her approach to work.

Sarah's story is more than just a practical example of how to use Copilot; it's a journey of growth. With each interaction, she learned to trust Copilot's suggestions, embrace automation for repetitive tasks, and use insights to make informed decisions. Sarah's experience shows us that Copilot isn't just about completing tasks faster; it's about empowering you to focus on what matters most, whether that's creative thinking, strategic planning, or meaningful collaboration.

Like Sarah, you may have started this journey wondering how Copilot could fit into your routine. But as you've seen, Copilot is here to lighten the load, help you get organized, and offer new ways to approach your work. Sarah's journey is a reminder that transforming the way we work takes time, experimentation, and a willingness to embrace new tools.

Just like Sarah, you now have the tools, insights, and best practices to continue your own journey with Copilot. This book has equipped you with practical knowledge to make Copilot an active part of your workflow. But beyond just using its features, you've gained an understanding of how Copilot can support your goals, streamline your projects, and help you achieve more each day.

With each prompt you give, every insight Copilot provides, and every task it helps you complete, you're taking a step toward transforming the way you work. You're not just saving time—you're opening up possibilities to focus on deeper, more impactful work. And that's the true power of Microsoft Copilot: it's a tool that adapts to you, supporting you as you continue to grow and achieve your goals.

As you continue exploring Copilot's features and expanding your skills, remember that this is a journey. Copilot will keep evolving, and so will your ability to use it creatively and confidently. Embrace the possibilities, experiment with prompts, and watch as Copilot helps you unlock new levels of productivity and insight.

Here's to your continued journey with Microsoft Copilot—a journey that's just beginning and filled with potential to redefine how you work, learn, and succeed.

A NEW WAY TO WORK WITH MICROSOFT COPILOT

Congratulations! You've reached the end of this journey into Microsoft Copilot, and now you're equipped with the tools and insights to truly make this powerful assistant your own. By exploring Copilot's features, mastering effective prompting, and applying best practices, you've transformed your approach to everyday tasks. Copilot is no longer just an add-on to your work—it's now an integral part of how you get things done, helping you work more efficiently, stay organized, and unlock new levels of productivity.

But this is just the beginning. Copilot is a tool designed to grow with you, adapting to your needs as they evolve. Whether you're working on complex projects, collaborating with a team, or simply organizing your day-to-day tasks, Copilot is here to support you every step of the way. With each interaction, you'll discover new ways it can simplify your workload, offer valuable insights, and free up time for the things that matter most.

Learning to work with Copilot is a journey in itself, one that will continue to unfold as you use it more. Just as you've seen in Sarah's story, growth doesn't stop here—it's an ongoing process of discovery and adaptation. The more you use Copilot, the better it will understand your needs, and the more effective it will become in helping you reach your goals.

As you continue, remember to:

- **Experiment and Explore**: Copilot's capabilities will keep expanding as Microsoft releases updates and new features. Stay curious, and don't hesitate to try out new prompts, test Copilot's responses, and see how it can tackle different tasks.

- **Build on Your Skills**: The prompting techniques, best practices, and tips you've learned here are tools you can take forward—not just with Copilot but with any AI tool you encounter. Embrace these skills and apply them wherever they can make your work easier.

- **Stay Open to New Possibilities**: Copilot isn't just a tool for efficiency; it's also a resource for creativity and inspiration. Let it support you in brainstorming ideas, exploring data, and making strategic decisions. The possibilities are as broad as your imagination.

Microsoft Copilot is part of a larger ecosystem in Microsoft 365, and as you become more comfortable with its capabilities, you might find yourself exploring how it integrates with other apps. Whether it's using Teams to collaborate more effectively, leveraging Excel for powerful data analysis, or organizing your projects with Planner, Copilot is here to enhance each experience.

This book has equipped you with everything you need to start, but your journey doesn't end with Copilot alone. The entire Microsoft 365 suite is filled with tools that, like Copilot, are designed to work smarter, adapt to your workflow, and support your goals. Embrace the opportunity to explore new apps, deepen your skills, and integrate these tools into your everyday work.

Every tool, every prompt, every insight from Copilot is an opportunity for growth. As you move forward, remember that Copilot is here to empower you to work more confidently, accomplish more with less stress, and bring creativity and focus into your daily tasks. Copilot isn't just about transforming how you work—it's about transforming what you're capable of achieving.

Thank you for taking this journey with us. Here's to the continued exploration, learning, and success that awaits you with Microsoft Copilot. May it be the assistant that adapts to your needs, the partner that supports your goals, and the tool that helps you redefine what's possible in your work.